I0017585

LOL Mechanics

LOL MECHANICS
Crafting Prank Game Features That Delight

Embracing the Magic of Prank Mechanics

The allure of prank mechanics in gaming resides in their remarkable ability to craft unexpected moments of joy and surprise, resonating deeply with our innate yearning for playfulness and humor. For product managers, grasping this enchantment is vital when designing captivating experiences that connect with players. Prank mechanics are a powerful bridge between traditional gameplay and community interaction, empowering developers to break the fourth wall and engage users in exciting and entertaining ways. This innovative approach fosters memorable moments that players eagerly share, nurturing a vibrant community and enhancing the gaming journey.

Their extraordinary capacity to subvert expectations is at the heart of practical prank mechanics. When players anticipate a particular outcome, a well-timed prank can completely flip that expectation, sparking laughter and amazement. This unpredictability shines particularly brightly in games as a service, where sustained engagement is essential. Developers can ignite enthusiasm by incorporating prank game mechanics during seasonal events, such as April Fools' Day, motivating players to log in and uncover new, humorous content. These experiences entertain and deepen player loyalty by showing that developers truly understand the community's craving for novelty.

Humorous in-game events wield immense power in nurturing player engagement. By weaving in satirical updates or absurd game features, developers can comment on gaming culture or industry trends while delighting their audience. Such features often lead to viral moments, as players enthusiastically share their adventures on social media, amplifying the prank's reach and impact. Product managers should thoughtfully harmonize these mechanics with existing game features to elevate the overall narrative and gameplay, ensuring a seamless experience that maintains player trust while boldly exploring creativity.

Beyond the fun factor, prank mechanics offer a clever avenue for monetization that respects the player base. Whimsical monetization strategies, like selling a fictitious expansion pack or offering comical game skins, can captivate interest and generate revenue while preserving a joyful spirit. By embedding these elements within the game's ongoing narrative, developers can foster a sense of enjoyment rather than exploitation.

This approach not only amplifies the game's humor but also cultivates a shared experience among players who appreciate the lighthearted nature of the offerings.

Finally, spirited community challenges rooted in prank mechanics can elevate player engagement and foster a collaborative atmosphere. Initiatives inviting players to create or share their prank ideas can unlock a treasure trove of user-generated content, enriching the game's ecosystem. This participatory spirit transforms players into active contributors, solidifying their connection to the game. As product managers delve into the realm of prank mechanics, embracing their appeal can unveil new pathways for creativity, community engagement, and, ultimately, player satisfaction.

The Evolution of Games as a Service

The concept of Games as a Service (GaaS) has redefined the gaming landscape, marking a remarkable transition from traditional one-time purchase models to dynamic service-oriented frameworks. Gone are the days of standalone products, as the digital marketplace has evolved alongside gamers' rising expectations, leading to the birth of GaaS. This innovative model empowers developers to engage players continuously through regular content updates, seasonal events, and community interactions, nurturing a loyal player base and creating sustainable revenue streams.

As GaaS has evolved, it has embraced elements of humor and satire, particularly within the realm of April Fools' Day events and playful mechanics. Developers have tapped into the understanding that players cherish lighthearted experiences, fostering engaging and humorous content that reflects the joyful spirit of gaming culture. Such events entertain and nurture community bonds, allowing players to feel like active contributors to a shared experience. This creative approach has ushered in imaginative expressions, including fake expansion packs and whimsical game features that serve as both marketing initiatives and delightful distractions.

The introduction of fictional game characters and comedic skins has flourished within GaaS, showcasing how humor can be woven into character design and gameplay. These elements often serve as insightful commentaries on the gaming industry, enabling developers to critique established tropes playfully. For instance, parody trailers have become a vibrant way to engage audiences, merging humor with marketing to generate excitement around new titles or updates.

Additionally, satirical game updates and exaggerated monetization strategies have emerged as quintessential aspects of the GaaS model. Developers create a humorous critique by amplifying standard practices within the industry, entertaining players while inviting engagement. This sparks community conversations about industry norms and fosters connections among players who appreciate this comedic lens. In embracing absurdity, developers highlight the unique quirks of gaming culture while courageously challenging prevailing monetization practices.

Lastly, playful community challenges have become essential in GaaS, inviting players to participate in whimsical events that encourage collaboration and friendly competition. These challenges incorporate humor, allowing players to interact with the game upliftingly. Developers can cultivate a vibrant ecosystem where players feel valued and inspired by fostering community engagement. Ultimately, the evolution of Games as a Service has unlocked new realms for creativity, enabling developers to design experiences that captivate players while reflecting on and transforming the gaming industry.

The Role of Humor in Gaming

Humor in gaming is more than just a source of entertainment; it's a powerful force that enriches player engagement and nurtures community interaction. In a world often dominated by serious narratives and fierce competition, the inclusion of humor offers a delightful escape. Witty dialogue, absurd game mechanics, and playful visual designs spark laughter and joy, crafting unforgettable gaming experiences. For product managers, recognizing the importance of integrating humor into game design is crucial for creating features that resonate with players and inspire lasting engagement.

One of the most impactful methods to introduce humor is through prank game mechanics. These surprises, filled with unexpected twists or ridiculous consequences, challenge player expectations in delightful ways. A simple quest can transform into an adventure full of exaggerated scenarios, such as a character morphing into a hilariously over-the-top version of themselves. This element of surprise not only elevates the unpredictability of the game but also sparks stories that gamers eagerly share, deepening community bonds. Product managers should thoughtfully balance humor with gameplay, ensuring player challenges remain engaging and entertaining.

Humorous in-game events also play a crucial role in generating a joyful atmosphere. Seasonal celebrations, like April Fools' Day, offer a unique opportunity to introduce temporary content that humorously critiques common gaming clichés or trends. A mock expansion pack touting outrageous features can create excitement and buzz, leading to an increase in player participation. These events break the routine of regular gameplay, fostering camaraderie among players as they collectively embrace the humor. Product managers should harness these moments to cultivate community and a sense of belonging, which is essential for player retention.

Fictional characters that embody humor can significantly boost player immersion. Comedic characters, with their exaggerated traits and whimsical backstories, can become cherished icons within the game universe. These figures often act as vessels for humor, delivering punchlines and engaging in hilarious antics that resonate deeply with players. By creating relatable comedic characters, product managers can forge strong emotional connections, inspiring loyalty and encouraging frequent engagement with game content.

Finally, the impact of humor in marketing strategies, through parody trailers or whimsical monetization tactics, is profoundly significant. Creative marketing using humor can attract potential players, inviting them to explore a game more deeply. By highlighting the humorous facets of gameplay and the playful spirit of the community, these marketing endeavors distinguish a game in a competitive landscape. Product managers should view humor as a central selling point, appealing to a diverse audience and nurturing a lively community around their creations. By embracing humor as a core design principle, game developers can craft experiences that captivate, inspire, and bring joy to players, nurturing a flourishing gaming ecosystem.

Planning Effective April Fools Events

Planning effective April Fools events can ignite creativity and elevate player engagement through a strategic and joyful approach. Product managers should embrace their game's core values and vibrant community culture. Understanding player preferences fosters the development of unique prank concepts that not only entertain but also strengthen community bonds. By analyzing past April Fools events in the gaming industry, managers can uncover invaluable insights that inspire innovative ideas tailored to the game's distinctive tone.

When brainstorming prank game mechanics, consider infusing surprising and delightful elements. Imagine creating fake game expansion packs that promise outrageous features or absurd characters that defy expectations. A cleverly timed introduction of a fictional game character can enchant players and provide light-hearted commentary on game tropes, encouraging interaction and creating lasting memories that players will cherish long after the event ends.

Humorous in-game events should engage players organically, fostering a harmonious blend of play and laughter; rather than simply adding a funny skin or feature, design scenarios that allow players to participate in the prank on multiple levels. A satirical game update might introduce a whimsical power-up that momentarily transforms characters into hilarious versions of themselves, sparking camaraderie and shared joy among players.

Incorporating parody game trailers serves as a promotional tool and a celebration of creativity for April Fools events. These trailers can playfully exaggerate game elements while cleverly poking fun at industry trends, capturing attention, and sparking conversations. By weaving humor into marketing efforts, product managers can create excitement around the game, drawing in passionate players and newcomers who appreciate clever satire.

Lastly, playful community challenges can amplify player involvement and spread excitement surrounding the event. Inviting players to submit their absurd ideas for monetization strategies or ridiculous features fosters creativity and engagement. This collaborative spirit allows the community to contribute, generating a treasure trove of user-generated content that thrives on social media. Through this embrace of collaboration and fun, April Fools events can become a highlight in the gaming calendar, cultivating lasting player loyalty and enjoyment.

Case Studies of Successful Prank Games

Case studies of successful prank games illuminate effective design choices and player engagement strategies that resonate powerfully within the gaming community. One example is the April Fools' event from a significant multiplayer online battle arena game. This event introduced an unforgettable mechanic where players could temporarily transform into inanimate objects like bushes or barrels. This surprise delivered comedic delight and encouraged players to explore unconventional strategies, ultimately enriching social interactions and crafting cherished community moments.

Another inspiring case involved a fictitious game expansion pack that humorously critiqued conventional DLC offerings. This "expansion" boasted hilariously exaggerated features, like an endless array of new skins—some delightfully impractical and others nonsensical. One beloved character was transformed into a giant rubber duck, and the sheer absurdity triggered vibrant discussions across social media platforms, showcasing how humor can critique and captivate, drawing in players and boosting retention.

In humorous in-game events, a well-known sandbox game executed a prank mechanic where players encountered "glitches" that turned out to be elaborate jokes. These ranged from characters dancing unexpectedly to whimsical changes in environments, such as gravity-defying landscapes. This event ignited enthusiasm and inspired players to share their joyful experiences, creating a surge of user-generated content. This case exemplifies the power of playful elements in enhancing player engagement and generating excitement, ultimately sustaining long-term interest.

Parody game trailers also prove to be

an effective channel for connecting with players through humor. One memorable trailer boldly spoofed the over-the-top marketing tactics often seen in gaming. By creatively exaggerating familiar tropes, the trailer resonated with players, leaving a lasting impact and reinforcing the joy that can be found in playful storytelling.

Metrics for Measuring Success in Prank Game Design

In the exciting world of prank game design, effective metrics for measuring success empower product managers to create unforgettable and engaging experiences. These metrics extend beyond traditional performance indicators, diving deeply into the unique and playful aspects of prank mechanics. By understanding how players interact with humorous in-game events and respond to satirical updates, invaluable insights can emerge, revealing the true impact of these features.

Player feedback is an essential metric, gathered through surveys or in-game analytics. This qualitative data shines a light on player sentiments about specific prank elements, such as the reception of absurd game features or comical skins. Analyzing player comments and ratings helps product managers gauge the effectiveness of humor, paving the way for future enhancements. Additionally, monitoring social media channels fosters a wider view of a prank's community impact, showcasing which elements truly resonate with players.

Engagement metrics, including session length and the number of active users during prank events, serve as clear indicators of a feature's success. A fake game expansion that increases session times or spikes daily active users demonstrates the power of a well-executed prank. Conversely, a drop in engagement points to opportunities for growth and improvement. Tracking these metrics over time reveals trends and patterns, enabling product managers to refine their strategies for future releases.

Retention rates following prank features reflect whether players find lasting value in their gaming experience. Players who return after enjoying a humorous event or a parody trailer signify that the prank has enriched their journey. In contrast, a high churn rate post-event may highlight that while the prank entertained, it may not have fostered long-term satisfaction. By examining retention alongside player feedback, product managers can uncover the keys to lasting engagement.

Finally, monetization strategies linked to prank mechanics deserve careful evaluation. Metrics such as revenue from comedic in-game purchases or the success of promotional events reveal players' willingness to embrace absurd features. Striking the right balance between humor and monetization is essential, ensuring that the playful spirit of the game shines through. By continually assessing these metrics, product managers can craft prank game features that not only thrill players but also propel the game to new heights of success.

Core Principles of Prank Mechanics

Core principles of prank mechanics in game design form the foundation for creating engaging and humorous experiences that resonate powerfully with players. By understanding these principles, product managers can craft features that entertain and ignite community engagement. The essence of prank mechanics lies in their capacity to surprise and delight players, often turning expectations upside down while nurturing a playful spirit. By delving into these core principles, game developers can create unforgettable moments that inspire players to share their experiences, enhancing the game's visibility and appeal.

The first principle is the element of surprise. Successful pranks thrive on the unexpected, catching players off guard while delivering joy. This can be achieved through sudden game events disrupting the usual gameplay flow or unforeseen interactions with game characters. For instance, introducing a fake game expansion that players initially believe to be genuine, only to unveil it as a satirical commentary on standard expansion pack tropes, can spark laughter and meaningful discussion within the community. This principle underscores the importance of timing and execution, ensuring the surprise is delightful and seamlessly integrated into the game experience.

Another critical principle is relatability. Pranks resonate more deeply when they mirror players' shared experiences or common challenges within the gaming community. By incorporating familiar gaming clichés or humorously exaggerated scenarios, developers can forge personal connections between players and the prank. A parody game trailer that humorously critiques popular game mechanics or features can create a sense of camaraderie among players who recognize the satire. Grounding pranks in relatable contexts enhance player engagement and social sharing, as players are more inclined to share experiences they find personally amusing or relevant.

The third principle is balance. While pranks are designed to be humorous, they must also protect the integrity of the game. Excessive or disruptive pranks can lead to frustration rather than enjoyment. Striking a balance between humor and gameplay ensures that pranks enhance the player experience. For instance, a humorous in-game event that temporarily alters mechanics or visual aesthetics can provide a refreshing twist without undermining core gameplay. This principle challenges product managers to consider the long-term impact of prank mechanics, ensuring they contribute positively to player retention and satisfaction.

Lastly, community involvement is a cornerstone of practical prank mechanics. Engaging players in the design and execution of pranks nurtures a sense of ownership and investment in the game. This can be achieved through community challenges where players submit their prank ideas or vote on potential humorous features. Incorporating user-generated content into prank mechanics enhances the sense of community and collaboration. By actively involving players in the prank design process, product managers can create experiences that reflect the collective humor and creativity of the player base, amplifying the prank's impact and strengthening community bonds.

Balancing Humor and Gameplay

Balancing humor and gameplay is essential for crafting engaging and memorable game experiences, mainly during April Fools' Day or other humorous events. Product managers must recognize that humor can elevate the gameplay experience but must be integrated carefully to avoid overshadowing core mechanics. A successful prank game feature should feel natural within the game's universe while delivering a lighthearted twist that surprises and delights players. This requires a considered approach to ensure that humor enhances rather than detracts from gameplay.

One effective way to achieve this balance is to anchor comedic elements in the established lore or mechanics of the game. By leveraging familiar characters or settings, product managers can create continuity that makes the humor feel organic. A fictional game character could adopt exaggerated traits or behaviors that enhance their personality while still aligning with the game's narrative. This reinforces player attachment and allows the humor to resonate deeper, as players are already invested in the characters and their journeys.

Incorporating absurd features or satirical updates can also provide engaging gameplay moments without compromising the overall experience. Players often appreciate the unexpected, and when these elements are introduced thoughtfully, they can lead to unforgettable interactions. For example, a parody game trailer that humorously misrepresents an expansion pack can generate excitement, drawing players in with its absurdity while still showcasing the actual game content.

User Engagement Strategies

User engagement is a vital element in designing and executing prank game features that not only entertain but also cultivate a devoted community. Product managers have the opportunity to explore innovative strategies that inspire players to interact with the game in significant ways. One powerful approach is to introduce humorous in-game events that delight players and break the routine of traditional gameplay. Timing these events with real-world occasions, such as April Fools' Day, can amplify their impact through shared cultural relevance. By crafting events that invite players to immerse themselves in absurd scenarios, developers can enhance engagement while fostering an atmosphere of playful unpredictability.

Another inspiring strategy focuses on incorporating fictional game characters that resonate deeply with players. Designing these characters with exaggerated traits or humorous backgrounds encourages players to connect and share their experiences. By weaving a narrative that aligns with the prank elements of the game, product managers can create a rich context for engagement. Players are naturally inclined to discuss and promote these characters through social media and community forums, generating authentic buzz and sustaining interest in the game over time.

To further inspire user engagement, developers can harness the creativity of parody game trailers that humorously mock existing gaming trends or popular titles. Such trailers not only act as promotional tools but also ignite discussions among players about the gaming industry. By positioning the game within a familiar context, players are more likely to share these trailers within their networks, effectively expanding the game's reach. This strategy shines when combined with satirical game updates that playfully critique common gaming tropes or mechanics, encouraging players to experience the humor firsthand.

Moreover, introducing absurd game features can spark community interaction. By implementing mechanics that challenge conventional gameplay, product managers can create excitement among players eager to experiment and share their discoveries. Features like outrageous game monetization strategies or playful community challenges invite collaboration and competition, enriching the overall gaming experience. When players feel they are part of a community that embraces humor and creativity, they are more inclined to remain engaged and invested in the game's future.

Lastly, maintaining regular communication with the player base through social media and in-game messaging is essential for nurturing engagement. By seeking feedback on potential prank game mechanics or humorous updates, product managers can foster a sense of ownership among players. This collaborative spirit strengthens community ties and ensures that content remains relevant and enjoyable. By continuously evolving the game in response to player input, developers can cultivate an engaging environment that keeps players inspired and coming back for more, ultimately leading to a vibrant and thriving gaming community.

Conceptualizing Absurd Expansions

Imagining absurd expansions for prank games opens a vibrant door to blending humor with innovative gameplay mechanics. These expansions thrive on the ability to subvert player expectations while delivering comedic experiences that resonate deeply with their sensibilities. Product managers must take on the responsibility of crafting features that are not only delightfully outrageous but also tactically designed to elicit laughter, enhance engagement, and ensure playability. Thorough understanding of the audience's unique sense of humor— alongside their appetite for the absurd—is crucial in this process.

One powerful avenue for conceptualizing these expansions is to draw inspiration from a myriad of existing cultural or gaming tropes, then intentionally push them into the realm of absurdity. For instance, one might envision a fictional expansion titled "Cats in Space" for a gritty military simulation game that is typically centered around realism and strategy. This whimsical twist would transform the game's tone, inviting players to engage in ludicrous missions involving space-faring felines equipped with laser collars and tactical catnip. This not only injects humor but also encourages players to see the game through a fresh lens, fostering a sense of community and shared experience as they bond over the absurdity.

Integrating satirical game updates significantly enhances the absurd aspect of these expansions. By playfully poking fun at popular gaming trends, such as loot boxes or battle passes, developers can create in-game events that lightheartedly critique these mechanisms. Imagine implementing a "Loot Box Lottery" where players receive hilariously extravagant and completely impractical rewards, such as an exorbitant sum of a million in-game currency for winning a single match, or a whimsical skin that transforms characters into giant rubber chickens complete with comical sound effects. Such self-aware humor not only entertains but also sparks critical thought among players regarding industry practices, pushing them to question and discuss these elements within the gaming community.

Comedic game skins and fictional characters are pivotal in amplifying the absurdity of these expansions. Product managers can utilize brainstorming sessions to create characters that epitomize the game's whimsical premise—imagine villainous avocados plotting world domination or heroic slices of toast embarking on epic quests. By designing skins that reflect these characters' playful nature—complete with exaggerated animations and humorous interactions—players are much more likely to engage with the content and share their amusing experiences on social media. This cultivates organic promotion and community involvement, as appreciation for absurdity thrives and encourages sharing among players.

Finally, embracing playful community challenges helps to keep players interacting in unexpected and joyous ways. Consider events that prompt players to complete silly tasks—such as collecting virtual rubber ducks scattered throughout the game world or engaging in dance-offs with quirky non-playable characters (NPCs). These lighthearted challenges cultivate a sense of camaraderie, ensuring that gameplay remains entertaining and carefree. Moreover, by tying these challenges to limited-time events, developers can generate a sense of urgency and excitement. By weaving humor into the gameplay's very core, product managers inspire a dedicated community eager to explore the next absurd expansion, ultimately creating a vibrant and engaged player base.

Marketing Fake Expansions

Marketing fake expansions presents an astute and entertaining strategy to engage players, especially during special occasions such as April Fools' Day. These playful pranks cleverly catch players off guard, generating an influx of buzz and excitement around a game, thereby significantly enhancing its longevity and overall appeal. For product managers, mastering the art of marketing these fake expansions becomes essential to leveraging humor and creativity, ultimately strengthening player loyalty and fostering a rich tapestry of community interaction.

To craft a compelling narrative for a fake expansion, it's vital to align it with the game's existing lore while wholeheartedly embracing the element of absurdity. Developing an engaging backstory filled with humorous elements invites players into this fictitious world. Imagine introducing fictional characters as protagonists, complete with exaggerated traits and ridiculous abilities— perhaps a clumsy robot with a quirky obsession for collecting old video game cartridges as part of its upgrade protocol. Such an approach enhances the comedic effect within promotional materials and resonates with fans' imaginations.

Amplifying the reach of these fake expansions through social media channels is crucial for capturing player interest. Engaging influencers within the gaming community to share the prank can significantly elevate visibility and reach. Creating parody trailers that mimic traditional game announcements —replete with over-the-top graphics, humorous commentary, and outlandish features—becomes a focal point for social media campaigns. These tongue-in-cheek trailers inspire players to share their reactions widely, bolstering community engagement and creating a shared experience around the absurdity.

Furthermore, incorporating humorous in-game events alongside the launch of the fake expansion creates a seamless and immersive experience. Implementing ridiculous challenges, such as racing to fill a comically oversized piñata with in-game items or hosting a scavenger hunt for outrageously whimsical items, aligns perfectly with the spirit of the prank while enhancing player enjoyment. Introduce limited-time events where players can collect items like inflatable unicorns or quirky hats that express joy and shared laughter. This not only brings added excitement to the gaming experience but also unites the community in reveling in the absurdity, making it all the more vibrant and alive.

Community Reactions and Feedback

Community reactions and feedback are essential catalysts that shape the success of prank game features within the ever-evolving landscape of Games as a Service (GaaS). Introducing playful elements, such as creatively themed April Fools' designs or satirical game updates, not only enhances the player experience but also offers a unique opportunity for deeper engagement. By tracking and analyzing player responses through various channels—such as dedicated forums, social media platforms, and in-game surveys—product managers can effectively gauge the pulse of the player base, leading to improved satisfaction and community cohesion.

Initial responses to prank game mechanics often reveal a broad spectrum of emotions among players. For example, while some players enthusiastically embrace the humor and creative ingenuity behind features such as whimsical in-game items or unexpected character skins, others may perceive these elements as distractions that detract from the core gameplay. Positive feedback typically emphasizes the joy and sense of community these cleverly executed features foster, showcasing instances where players share their favorite prank moments or engage in lighthearted competitions. Conversely, adverse reactions necessitate thoroughly examining how such elements affect gameplay dynamics, particularly balance and fairness. By rigorously analyzing this feedback, product managers can fine-tune their strategies, ensuring that future prank mechanics resonate well with the audience while nurturing the existing player community.

Moreover, community-driven feedback

often ignites unexpected innovations. Players frequently contribute imaginative ideas for humorous in-game events or eccentric features, leading developers to explore bold new directions. For example, fan-generated concepts like a "silly skins" contest or "prank week" events can inspire developers to integrate similar challenges into the game. When such community-driven challenges gain traction, product managers have the opportunity to harness that momentum, ensuring these concepts are seamlessly woven into the game's evolving fabric. This collaborative atmosphere enhances player engagement and cultivates a vibrant ecosystem where creativity flourishes, enabling prank game elements to develop organically.

The influence of parody game trailers and comedic game skins is particularly noteworthy. When crafted with intent and care, these features act as powerful marketing tools and provide community engagement channels. For instance, a well-executed parody trailer that humorously exaggerates game mechanics can generate excitement and buzz, appealing to current players and attracting new ones. Critical reception and feedback from the community provide invaluable insights that help product managers refine their marketing strategies and tailor future content to align with player preferences. A successful parody trailer can reveal specific types of humor that resonate deeply with the audience, guiding the development of promotional materials and in-game content.

Ultimately, the community's reactions to unconventional monetization strategies and outlandish expansion packs offer invaluable lessons in balancing humor and player expectations. While certain players might appreciate a lighthearted and transparent approach to monetization—such as providing fun cosmetic items at a reasonable price—others may feel exploited if the line is blurred, significantly when these features disrupt gameplay. Product managers can adeptly navigate this delicate terrain by attentively monitoring discussions and sentiment across various platforms, ensuring they maintain player satisfaction without sacrificing humor. Embracing community reactions and fostering open dialogue empowers an engaged player base and creates a vibrant gaming ecosystem, transforming prank features into essential components of ongoing player interaction and enjoyment.

Creating Memorable Events in Games as a

Service

Creating memorable events within games as a service presents an exciting opportunity to blend creativity, humor, and a deep understanding of player psychology. Product managers can harness these elements to design inventive features that engage players and foster a vibrant sense of community. The true magic of a successful event lies in its ability to surprise and delight players, crafting unforgettable moments that they are eager to share with friends. By embracing playful themes and satirical content, these events can significantly enhance the overall gaming experience while promoting lasting user engagement.

When designing humorous in-game events, aligning the theme with the game's narrative, mechanics, and artistic style is crucial. Introducing fictional characters that cleverly parody popular genre tropes and industry conventions can create an immediate connection with players. These characters, overflowing with exaggerated traits—such as a bumbling hero with grandiose aspirations or a villain who comically misunderstands their evil plans—invite laughter and enjoyment. Incorporating absurd game features, like nonsensical mechanics (e.g., gravity-defying jumps or oddly complex crafting recipes) or ludicrous tasks (such as collecting quirky, fictional items), can amplify the hilarity and encourage enthusiastic player participation.

Satirical game updates provide another compelling strategy for crafting memorable events. By playfully critiquing common industry practices, such as excessive monetization or convoluted storylines, product managers can engage players in a friendly dialogue while nurturing community bonds. For instance, a fictional game expansion pack that humorously exaggerates the nature of downloadable content (DLC) with over-the-top pricing or absurdly unnecessary features can spark insightful conversations among players about their personal experiences with monetization strategies. These updates not only entertain but also cultivate a shared appreciation for gaming culture, strengthening connections within the community.

To further enrich the impact of these events, utilizing comedic game skins and parody trailers can be exceptionally effective. Transforming beloved characters into outrageous versions of themselves—like turning a stoic warrior into a flamboyant fashionista—adds a layer of joy to gameplay. Additionally, parody trailers that humorously mimic popular movie trailers or iconic game launches can generate excitement and anticipation leading up to the event's launch.

By placing humor at the forefront of these promotional materials, product managers can inspire player engagement and encourage participation in community challenges that amplify the event's reach and overall impact.

Ultimately, creating memorable events is about crafting experiences that players will treasure long after the event concludes. By focusing on surprise, humor, and community interaction, product managers can develop innovative prank game mechanics—such as unexpected twists in quests or fun player-versus-environment challenges that play with established norms—that resonate deeply with their audience. These events provide entertainment and nurture a vibrant gaming community where players feel connected to both the game and one another through shared laughter, joy, and a collective sense of belonging.

Timing and Execution

Timing and execution are pivotal elements in crafting prank game features, particularly within the evolving landscape of Games as a Service (GaaS). April Fools' Day is a prime opportunity for product managers to engage players through clever humor and joyful experiences. Launching prank features at optimal moments enhances both anticipation and excitement within the gaming community, creating a shared experience that brings players together. However, execution goes beyond just technical deployment; it must integrate communication strategies that genuinely resonate with players, developing a sense of community and connection.

Creating prank game mechanics invites us to think broadly about timing, considering not just the calendar but also the nuances of the game's lifecycle and player engagement patterns. By strategically incorporating a delightful prank into a seasonal event or a major game update, it transforms into a seamless and innovative extension of gameplay. Product managers can analyze player behavior data—such as peak engagement periods, in-game interactions, and community sentiment—to unlock the ideal timing for these features, ensuring they achieve optimal visibility and interaction within the player base.

Execution embodies a delicate balance of humor and respect for our diverse player base. The goal is to cultivate joy and surprise while consistently honoring the integrity of the gaming experience. For instance, a humorous, fake game expansion should be accompanied by a comprehensive communication strategy that clarifies its playful intent. This transparency fosters trust and enhances the overall experience, allowing players to fully appreciate the humor without feeling misled. Additionally, real-time monitoring of player reactions—through analytics, social media trends, and community feedback—empowers us to adapt and refine our approach as necessary, ensuring players feel heard and engaged.

Incorporating whimsical in-game events or satirical updates requires meticulous planning and coordination. Synchronizing these events with community activity, such as player milestones or significant in-game achievements, amplifies their impact. Aligning a comedic event with a game anniversary or a widely recognized trend can generate considerable buzz and encourage widespread participation and discussion within the community. Moreover, the execution phase involves creating engaging content and ensuring technical aspects, such as server stability, visual design, and user interface, are optimized to handle a wave of excited players seeking to dive into the new experience.

Ultimately, establishing feedback loops is invaluable in our execution strategy. After rolling out prank features, actively engaging with the community through surveys, social media interactions, and direct feedback channels opens up pathways for crucial insights into successes and potential improvement areas. This feedback serves as the cornerstone for refining future prank mechanics, allowing the elements of timing and execution to continually evolve and align with player expectations. By prioritizing both aspects, product managers can craft engaging experiences that delight players and strengthen community bonds, fostering a vibrant and cohesive gaming environment.

Inspiring Player Engagement Analysis

Analyzing player engagement within prank game mechanics is an essential journey for product managers aiming to craft features that genuinely resonate with their audience. By thoroughly examining player motivations—such as the desire for humor, surprise, and social interaction—alongside their behaviors and emotional responses, we can illuminate the design and execution of captivating, humorous in-game events and satirical updates. This analysis informs the types of content that will engage players and enhance the overall game experience, transforming casual players into loyal fans. Evaluating player interactions with these elements empowers managers to refine their approach, ensuring that each experience is entertaining and fosters sustained engagement and retention over time.

Monitoring player feedback and community interactions emerges as a highly effective method for dissecting player engagement. Social media platforms—like Twitter and Reddit—are dedicated to gaming, and active community hubs such as Discord or dedicated game subreddits serve as valuable resources for gauging player sentiment. By gathering qualitative insights from player discussions and quantitative data from engagement metrics, managers can uncover which prank features captivate players, spark joy, or, conversely, which aspects may require rethinking or improvement. This continuous feedback loop allows for real-time adjustments, enabling product managers to keep prank mechanics vibrant, fresh, and relevant to the evolving tastes of the player base.

Furthermore, a nuanced examination of in-game metrics is essential in this analytical endeavor. Product managers should utilize advanced analytics tools to meticulously track player behaviors concerning prank game features—such as the participation rates in limited-time humorous events, the frequency of comedic skin usage, and the duration of player engagement with these elements. Understanding player interaction patterns reveals preferences and trends, illuminating opportunities for production and development. For example, suppose certain absurd game elements, like outlandish character costumes or unexpected plot twists, drive higher player retention during specific events. In that case, managers can prioritize similar innovations in upcoming updates or expansions.

A/B testing is a strategy for exploring player engagement with specific prank mechanics. Product managers can effectively discover which version elicits a more positive response by systematically introducing variations of a game feature—such as differing effects of a prank or alternate visual styles—to segmented player demographics. This method sheds light on what players find genuinely amusing and plays a crucial role in refining monetization strategies surrounding these captivating features. Analyzing conversion rates and player spending related to various comedic elements—such as in-game purchases related to prank items—will inform data-driven decisions that shape future game content and promotional efforts.

Lastly, nurturing a playful community atmosphere becomes essential for elevating engagement. Product managers should actively champion player-driven content initiatives, such as community challenges encouraging players to create prank mechanics, submit creative ideas, or even develop parody game trailers. Such engagement fosters a sense of ownership and deepens players' emotional connection to the game, simultaneously uncovering valuable insights into community values and interests. By rigorously assessing participation levels and analyzing the nature of community-generated content, product managers can extract profound insights on player engagement and design future offerings that harmonize with these enlightening insights, ultimately leading to a much richer and more engaging gaming experience.

Embracing Satire in Gaming

Satire in gaming serves as a potent instrument for both critique and entertainment, particularly within the evolving landscape of games as a service. By skillfully harnessing the nuanced wit of satire, developers can thoughtfully tackle pressing industry trends, player behaviors, and contemporary cultural phenomena, while simultaneously delighting their audience with sharp humor. This distinctive approach enables product managers to craft interactive experiences that resonate deeply with players, transforming mere enjoyment into a reflective and thought-provoking journey. A nuanced understanding of satire's intricacies not only enhances the effectiveness of prank game features, but also ensures that these components connect meaningfully with the community, delivering punchlines that reflect the current gaming discourse.

Incorporating satirical elements into games necessitates a keen awareness of the audience's expectations, cultural sensitivities, and historical context. Product managers must deftly navigate the delicate line between humor and offense, especially since satire often seeks to challenge and question established norms. This understanding is essential when designing prank game mechanics or creating faux expansion packs that parody popular existing titles. By exaggerating familiar gameplay elements or spotlighting certain game features with wit, developers can shine a light on the industry's absurdities. Such exaggerations not only entertain but also inspire players to reflect on their own experiences and the broader gaming landscape.

Humorous in-game events and satirical updates present fantastic opportunities for engaging the community. By introducing fictional game characters that embody hyperbolic stereotypes or through playful skins that cleverly twist familiar tropes, developers can create memorable interactions that encourage players to share and discuss their experiences. These events are often strategically aligned with real-world happenings, such as April Fools' Day, where the inherent absurdity of gaming conventions is celebrated in a lighthearted manner. This strategy not only fosters a sense of community spirit but also reinforces the idea that gaming can serve as an impactful platform for meaningful social commentary.

Parody game trailers and ludicrous game features thrive on a satirical approach. Crafting trailers that cleverly mimic popular promotional styles while infusing humor and absurdity can effectively captivate audience attention and ignite excitement. Additionally, presenting farcical monetization strategies as satire challenges and provokes discussions about current industry practices. For instance, showcasing exaggerated paywalls or ludicrous in-game purchases highlights issues of fairness and ethics in the gaming industry, all while entertaining and engaging the audience.

Ultimately, embracing satire in gaming equips product managers with essential tools to forge compelling and unforgettable player experiences. By weaving humor into the very fabric of game design—whether through entertaining community challenges, humorous narratives, or satirical updates—developers can significantly elevate player engagement and cultivate a vibrant, interactive community. Acceptance and integration of satire not only enrich the gaming experience but also inspire players to think critically about the medium itself, ensuring that games continue to evolve as dynamic and innovative forms of entertainment that reflect and engage with ongoing cultural shifts.

Implementing Satirical Updates in Games as a Service

Implementing satirical updates within the games as a service (GaaS) model can significantly elevate player engagement and infuse the gaming experience with a refreshing and entertaining twist. These playful updates can take various forms, including humorous seasonal events, parody trailers that mimic well-known titles, or absurd game mechanics that poke fun at industry standards. Product managers must align these satirical elements with the game's core values while ensuring they resonate with the target player base. This alignment helps preserve brand integrity and opens avenues for creative experimentation, ultimately leading to memorable moments and increased player retention.

An effective strategy for deploying these satirical updates involves introducing fake expansion packs that cleverly reflect popular gaming trends or highly anticipated releases within the industry. For instance, a game could launch a faux expansion titled "Fantasy Farm Simulation" that comically combines elements of farming simulators with over-the-top fantasy quests. Crafting content that initially appears legitimate yet subverts player expectations through humor or absurdity can create heightened excitement within the gaming community. Such updates illuminate the ridiculousness of certain gaming tropes, thereby fostering a communal experience among players who appreciate and share in the satire.

Humorous in-game events can be strategically timed to coincide with real-world occasions, such as April Fools' Day or notable game anniversaries. These events might feature limited-time game modes, such as a "Reverse Difficulty Challenge," where players must make the game purposely easier, or through outrageous character skins that exaggerate existing game lore, such as a ninja dressed as a giant slice of pizza. Product managers can achieve success by meticulously balancing humor with gameplay mechanics, thus ensuring that these entertaining updates still deliver a satisfying and engaging experience for players. Incorporating community feedback into these updates can deepen their resonance; players often appreciate when their suggestions are transformed into comedic features within the game.

Additionally, satirical game updates can introduce fictional characters designed to embody the eccentricities of gaming culture. These characters, such as a quirky quest-giver with an exaggerated obsession for loot boxes or a sarcastic rival who critiques player strategies, can provide insightful commentary on player behavior and current industry trends. By crafting characters with vibrant personalities and ludicrous backstories, product managers can facilitate memorable interactions that players will remember and discuss long after the updates conclude. This approach enriches the game world and serves as a humorous critique of prevalent gaming stereotypes.

Lastly, employing outlandish monetization strategies as satire offers a unique and entertaining critique of player spending habits. For example, the introduction of fictitious in-game purchases, such as a "Cosmic Unicorn Skin Pack" priced at an exorbitant value or a subscription model promising access to "exclusive" non-existent content, can ignite discussions about the ethical implications surrounding monetization practices within the gaming industry. These satirical reflections can raise players' awareness about industry norms and encourage a more thoughtful approach to spending. Ultimately, the goal is to create a delightful experience that resonates with players, inviting them to engage with the game actively and appreciate the humor artfully woven into its updates.

Evaluating Impact on Player Base

Evaluating the impact of prank game features on the player base serves as a cornerstone for product managers eager to elevate engagement and satisfaction. The introduction of whimsical April Fools' designs, parody game trailers, and lighthearted in-game events can profoundly shape player perception and participation. By understanding how these playful features resonate with players, we can refine future updates and ensure these elements enhance the gaming experience. Metrics such as player retention, engagement rates, and social media interactions give invaluable insights into how these delightful quirks are embraced.

One powerful approach to gauge the impact of prank mechanics is through player feedback and community sentiment analysis. Surveys, forums, and social media channels become vibrant platforms for players to share their opinions and experiences. Collecting qualitative data on how players perceive absurd game features and humorous monetization strategies empowers product managers to pinpoint the elements that resonate most. Additionally, monitoring discussions about fictional characters and comedic skins unveils trends that can inspire future design choices.

Quantitative metrics are equally vital in evaluating player base impact. Analyzing engagement statistics, such as the number of active users during humorous events or sales figures for fake expansion packs, provides solid evidence of how these features shape player behavior. By comparing data from before and after the introduction of comedic elements, product managers can measure the success of their strategies and adapt as needed. This data-driven approach ensures that prank designs meaningfully enhance the overall player experience.

Moreover, understanding the demographic and psychographic profiles of the player base is essential. Different segments may respond uniquely to prank game mechanics, resulting in diverse impacts on engagement. For instance, younger audiences might delight in satirical updates, while seasoned players may prefer subtler humor. Tailoring content to meet the expectations and preferences of various player segments can amplify the effectiveness of prank game features, ensuring they bring joy rather than alienation.

Ultimately, evaluating the impact of

prank game features calls for a holistic approach that blends qualitative insights with quantitative data. By continually monitoring player reactions and behaviors in response to playful features and community challenges, product managers can refine their strategies. This iterative process not only enriches the player experience but also fosters a vibrant and engaged community, ensuring that prank game mechanics remain a cherished aspect of the gaming landscape.

Designing Comedic Characters

Designing comedic characters is an essential element in creating engaging prank game features that resonate deeply with players on both an emotional and playful level. These characters serve not only as the face of your game but also as conduits for humor, enriching the overall player experience and fostering a sense of connection. The core of successful comedic character design lies in thoroughly understanding your audience's unique sense of humor, allowing you to create diverse personalities that beautifully align with the whimsical and light-hearted nature of your game. Product managers can inspire genuine joy by ensuring these characters are relatable yet exaggerated, striking a harmonious balance that invites laughter while fostering player engagement.

When developing these comedic personas, consider harnessing classic archetypes that enhance humor through well-known tropes. Characters such as the bumbling fool—who consistently trips over their own feet at the worst possible moments, the overconfident hero—who has an inflated sense of self-worth yet hilariously fails to complete even the simplest tasks, or the overly serious antagonist—whose stern demeanor is completely at odds with their ridiculous schemes, can be infused with unexpected comedic twists that delight players by subverting established expectations. Imagine a character who perceives themselves as the ultimate prankster but finds that their elaborate plans frequently backfire in the most absurd ways, creating a never-ending source of laughter and entertainment.

Visual design plays a pivotal role in character creation, as it significantly impacts how players perceive and connect with the humor portrayed. Comedic characters should feature pronounced and exaggerated traits that vividly showcase their distinct personalities. For instance, oversized heads can amplify their expressions of surprise or dismay, while quirky outfits and outrageous accessories—notably flamboyant hats or mismatched shoes—can instantly communicate their humorous essence. Additionally, facial expressions and body language should be deliberately crafted to evoke laughter, whether through exaggerated reactions during shocking in-game moments or through cleverly executed slapstick antics that keep players engaged. This visual representation must also align seamlessly with each character's backstory and role within the game, enabling players to easily identify with them and form meaningful connections.

Dialogue and voice acting are crucial in breathing life into these comedic characters, serving as a vehicle for their humor and personality to shine. Clever one-liners, brilliantly timed puns, and playful back-and-forth exchanges can transform a simple interaction into a memorable moment, leaving lasting impressions on players. Product managers should closely collaborate with skilled writers and talented voice actors to ensure that the humor resonates genuinely and aligns perfectly with each character's unique personality. Timing is everything; a well-placed comedic line can elevate a character's impact and create increasingly engaging and entertaining experiences for players.

Lastly, comedic characters should undergo development throughout the game to maintain player interest and investment.

Implementing humorous character arcs—where characters learn from their mistakes or continuously evolve their prank strategies—keeps gameplay fresh and dynamic. Introducing limited-time events or seasonal updates that spotlight these characters ensures they remain relevant and intriguing. Moreover, by incorporating community feedback and actively involving players in character development, product managers can cultivate a vibrant and dynamic environment where comedic characters thrive, ultimately enhancing the game's overall appeal and longevity.

Integrating Characters into Gameplay

Integrating characters into gameplay is a transformative aspect of designing engaging and unforgettable experiences, particularly within prank game mechanics. For product managers focusing on games as a service, the skillful incorporation of fictional characters into gameplay can significantly enhance user engagement and satisfaction. Characters evolve from mere avatars into vibrant conduits of humor, satire, and delightful absurdity—qualities that are essential for crafting successful April Fools' designs and playful in-game events.

To masterfully integrate characters,

developing a compelling backstory that aligns seamlessly with the game's overarching narrative and thematic elements is crucial. For instance, a character could be a quirky game designer who has "escaped" into their creation, embodying the spirit of whimsy and self-referential humor. This character would infuse depth into gameplay, allowing players to forge a meaningful emotional connection and invest themselves wholeheartedly in their gaming journey. A character that offers a humorous or satirical perspective on traditional gaming tropes can become a beacon of parody, inviting players to engage with the character and the game mechanics in an uplifting and light-hearted manner. This connection can be further amplified in promotional materials featuring comedic game skins, tongue-in-cheek storylines, or satirical updates, enhancing the character's significance in gameplay and marketing.

Incorporating absurd game features through characters can also elevate the playful spirit of a game. Picture a character who introduces ridiculously whimsical challenges—like a "Dance-Off" against NPCs that involves zany dance moves or a "Meme Battle" where players create humorous memes to win. Such transformations turn everyday gameplay mechanics into joyful experiences, igniting viral moments that resonate within the gaming community and sparking lively conversations. This interactive approach helps maintain a vibrant gameplay atmosphere, encouraging players to share their comical adventures across social media platforms and fostering robust community involvement.

Moreover, the character's role should transcend conventional gameplay mechanics; they can become the backbone of community challenges and events. You can cultivate a sense of urgency and excitement by crafting time-sensitive events—perhaps a "Pranksters' Tournament" where players compete in over-the-top trickery while using that character. These events, filled with prank-themed challenges or humorous competitions, resonate particularly well with the community's desire for novelty and interaction. Such strategies enrich the gameplay experience, nurture player retention, and foster a loyal player base who eagerly anticipates the next event.

Lastly, a thoughtful approach to monetization can thrive alongside these characters through premium content offerings. Options could include comedic game skins that add specialized animations or sounds or exclusive character-themed expansion packs that introduce new realms filled with absurd quests. By aligning these monetization strategies with the character's narrative and the inherent absurdity of the game, product managers can create a seamless and organic experience that not only delights players but also strengthens the playful essence of the game itself. This multifaceted approach ensures characters remain integral to every aspect of gameplay, from engagement and community building to revenue generation.

Fan Engagement with Fictional Characters

Fan engagement with fictional characters is essential in transforming the gaming experience, particularly within prank game mechanics and humorous content. These characters are the emotional core of the gameplay, turning ordinary mechanics into an unforgettable adventure. When designed with comedic intent, they introduce layers of wit, absurdity, and satire that linger in players' minds long after they log out. This deep emotional connection fosters a vibrant community dedicated to prank features and encourages discussions that extend beyond the game itself.

Incorporating fictional characters into April Fools' designs can captivate fans and create memorable moments. By adeptly parodying well-known tropes or poking fun at familiar gaming clichés—such as exaggerated archetypes like the overly righteous hero or the scheming villain—these characters provide a refreshing and humorous perspective that resonates with players. For instance, imagine a character that comically amplifies the traits of a classic hero, donning an excessively flamboyant costume and delivering delightfully corny one-liners, becoming the face of a playful fake expansion pack. This narrative entertains and inspires players to share their whimsical experiences across social media platforms, significantly extending the game's reach through user-generated content, memes, and fan art.

Moreover, humorous in-game events featuring these fictional characters ignite deeper player engagement. Designing scenarios where characters find themselves embroiled in absurd situations—like competing in overly elaborate mini-games or embarking on hilarious satirical quests—encourages player interaction and community involvement. For example, a seasonal event might feature characters dressed as various pop culture icons, facing off in ludicrous challenges such as "The Great Gourmet Cook-Off," where the stakes are as absurd as the reward itself. Players are often more inclined to dive into events showcasing beloved characters, especially when infused with unexpected humor and unpredictable twists, creating a sense of camaraderie as they bond over shared experiences and strategies to conquer these whimsical challenges.

Comedic game skins and parody game trailers further enrich fan engagement through fictional characters. A character's design can reflect current trends, social issues, or pop culture, offering playful commentary that resonates deeply with the audience. Parody trailers featuring these characters can generate excitement and anticipation for upcoming game updates or events, using humor to maintain player interest and engagement. Witnessing their favorite characters in ludicrous situations—such as attempting to participate in a yoga retreat only to cause chaos inadvertently—fosters a shared experience that deepens their connection to both the game and its community.

Finally, even the integration of outrageous monetization strategies can cleverly involve fictional characters without alienating players. Introducing limited-time offers featuring absurdly themed skins—like a space-themed outfit for a traditionally earthbound character—creates genuine excitement and urgency among the player base. When players engage with these characters through amusing challenges or humorous content, they perceive monetization efforts as enjoyable enhancements rather than intrusive tactics.

This approach drives revenue and strengthens the bond between players and their beloved characters, ultimately enriching the gaming experience in profound and lasting ways.

The Art of Humorous Design

Integrating humor into game design, mainly through innovative prank game mechanics, is a transformative art that has the potential to elevate player engagement and create memorable gaming experiences significantly. When executed with creativity and a clear understanding of the audience, humorous design captivates players and fosters a vibrant sense of community among them. This subchapter invites product managers to delve into the essential principles of blending humor into various game features, enabling them to craft experiences that resonate deeply with their audience while maintaining the integrity of gameplay.

A fundamental aspect of the humorous design is achieving the delicate balance between absurdity and relatability—games as a service benefit immensely from dynamic updates that invigorate content and keep players returning. Developers delightfully subvert player expectations by introducing playful, fictitious expansion packs or satirical game updates. For instance, unveiling an extravagant expansion themed around a seemingly mundane concept, like "The Great Coffee Run," can spark joyous laughter while cleverly mocking familiar expansion tropes such as grandiose quests and epic storylines. This approach captures player interest and inspires them to share their hilarious adventures across social platforms, enhancing community bonds and engagement.

Moreover, comedic game skins and fictional characters present another thrilling avenue for humorous design. Crafting skins that parody trending popular culture references or iconic characters can evoke a sense of nostalgia and elicit genuine laughter. Product managers should pay close attention to how these skins reflect current trends or cultural nuances, ensuring they are timely and relevant to the player demographic. For example, introducing a character that personifies an overused gaming cliché, such as the "Overpowered Sidekick" or the "Stereotypical Mage," serves as a humorous critique of common stereotypes in gaming narratives, enriching both the storytelling aspect and gameplay while illuminating the inherent absurdities of certain conventions.

In addition, engaging players through humorous in-game events and whimsical community challenges can significantly energize the player base. Seasonal events—particularly around April Fools' Day—present the perfect opportunity to implement surprise-laden prank mechanics that enchant players and keep them laughing. A community challenge encouraging participants to complete ludicrous objectives, such as "Collect 100 Llamas in 24 Hours" or participate in an outrageous scavenger hunt, fosters a shared experience that unites players in lighthearted joy. Such events enhance overall engagement and promote social interaction in a collaborative and entertaining atmosphere.

Finally, product managers should recognize the extraordinary potential of parody game trailers and whimsical monetization strategies within humorous design. Crafting a trailer that comically exaggerates the features of an upcoming release—perhaps by showcasing absurdly over-the-top combat scenes or ludicrously unrealistic gameplay elements—serves as a clever marketing strategy that grabs attention and sets the tone for the humor players can expect. Incorporating outrageous monetization tactics—such as selling virtual air, "exclusive" invisible items, or even comical luxury items like "Gold Plated Rubber Duckies"—can amuse players and critique prevalent industry practices. By embracing a humorous lens in monetization, developers can foster goodwill among players, transforming an often-continuous topic into a source of collective joy and shared laughter, ultimately enriching the player experience.

Monetization of Comedic Skins

The monetization of comedic skins has emerged as a dynamic and vibrant strategy within the gaming industry, mainly thriving in games structured as a service model. Product managers possess a unique opportunity to leverage these skins as aesthetic enhancements and joyful expressions that foster a sense of community and connection among players. By introducing imaginative skin designs that elicit joy and surprise—such as costumes that parody popular culture or whimsical transformations that defy reality—developers can cultivate deeper player investment and create a thriving ecosystem centered on humor and absurdity. This approach embodies the core principles of games as a service, where sustained engagement and player retention are crucial for fostering long-term loyalty.

Integrating prank-inspired gameplay mechanics into the monetization strategy further enhances the appeal of comedic skins. For example, skins that whimsically alter character appearances—like a knight dressed as a jester or a terrifying monster with oversized, colorful glasses—can infuse gameplay with an enjoyable lightheartedness. Such playful absurdity naturally attracts players, who are entertained by their avatars and motivated to share this experience on social media platforms, fostering organic word-of-mouth marketing. The opportunity to showcase these distinctive skins during gameplay encourages meaningful interactions among players, invigorating the community and maintaining a dynamic, engaged player base.

Another innovative monetization method is the development of mock game expansion packs that feature comedic skins and themes. By framing these expansions as enticing new content—with quirky narratives that poke fun at game tropes—developers can generate excitement and curiosity within their player demographics. It is essential to prioritize execution; the designs must be boldly imaginative, satirical, and reflective of the community's shared humor. Marketing materials should capture and highlight the essence of these humorous expansions, inviting players to indulge in the sheer joy they bring to the gaming experience.

In addition, hosting humorous in-game events is an excellent platform for showcasing comedic skins while effectively driving monetization efforts. Limited-time events, such as seasonal festivals or themed challenges, featuring unique rewards and exclusive themed skins create a sense of urgency and exhilaration that compels players to participate. Players are more likely to invest in comedic skins to fully engage with these events, where they can unlock exclusive items, achievements, or community recognition. By strategically aligning the release of these skins with engaging, vibrant events, product managers can tap into the playful essence of their player base, encouraging joyful spending while enriching their overall gaming experience.

Finally, creating parody game trailers and whimsical promotional features can amplify comedic skins' appeal and visibility. These marketing materials should reflect the skins' lighthearted spirit and creative essence, effectively capturing the imagination of potential new players and generating excitement within the gaming community. By embracing satirical updates, playful challenges, and humorous storytelling, product managers can formulate a comprehensive monetization strategy that boosts revenue and enhances the overall player experience. This fosters a vibrant community that celebrates the joy, creativity and shared laughter that gaming uniquely offers.

Community Reception and Trends

Community reception stands as a crucial pillar in the success of prank game features, playing a significant role in shaping player engagement and determining the effectiveness of these elements within a game-as-a-service (GaaS) model. Embracing player feedback is not just beneficial; it is essential, as it offers nuanced insights into how various prank mechanics resonate with different segments of the player base. The spectrum of responses—from enthusiastic praise for clever implementations that surprise and delight to pointed critiques of perceived insincerity or overreach—guides the creative journey of product managers. To effectively gauge these sentiments, a thorough monitoring of social media channels, gaming forums, and in-game communications is vital. By tapping into this pulse of the community, product managers can refine and enhance future prank elements that truly resonate.

Current trends within the gaming community showcase a growing appetite for humor and absurdity, reflecting a cultural shift in player preferences. Players increasingly celebrate game designs that challenge traditional conventions and invite a playful, sometimes irreverent spirit into gameplay. This shift has paved the way for engaging in-game events, including April Fools' Day specials and satirical content updates that humorously critique prevailing industry norms or tropes. Product managers can leverage this vibrant energy by integrating engaging elements that resonate deeply with players, such as eccentric game characters, whimsical scenarios, or parody trailers that creatively redefine traditional marketing approaches.

The introduction of comedic game skins and whimsical features has demonstrated a remarkable ability to enhance player retention and engagement. When players share their experiences with these delightful elements—be it a skin that comically exaggerates a character's traits or a feature that introduces an entirely fantastical experience—it fosters a community spirit rooted in humor and shared enjoyment. By designing skins that amplify specific character traits or introduce fantastical, unexpected elements, product managers can create memorable experiences that players are eager to discuss and promote. This organic word-of-mouth marketing can significantly elevate the game's visibility and allure, underscoring the critical importance of understanding community responses.

Furthermore, unconventional monetization strategies can spark spirited debates within the community. While some players find humor in creative pricing models or faux expansion packs that parody industry standards—such as limited-time offers or misleading promotions—others might express concerns over perceived exploitation or the game's integrity. This dynamic presents a unique opportunity for product managers to engage directly with their audience, nurturing proactive conversations that can yield innovative solutions. By attentively observing community reactions and sentiments, product managers can fine-tune their monetary approaches, ensuring players feel valued and appreciated while simultaneously enhancing their overall enjoyment.

Lastly, community-driven challenges infused with playful elements serve to strengthen bonds between players and the game itself. These challenges not only inspire participation but also empower players to express their creativity through engaging interactions with prank mechanics. Product managers should prioritize crafting challenges that encourage collaboration among players and foster a sense of friendly competition. By accurately aligning these initiatives with prevailing trends and genuine player feedback, they can cultivate a vibrant ecosystem that thrives on humor and community engagement, ultimately setting the stage for lasting success in the world of prank games.

Crafting Effective Parody Trailers

Crafting effective parody trailers is an imaginative and captivating approach to engaging your audience while seamlessly infusing humor into your marketing strategy. These trailers offer product managers a unique opportunity to creatively satirize well-known gaming tropes, current industry trends, or even specific elements of their games. By doing so, they cultivate an environment filled with laughter, surprise, and community among players. A thoughtfully executed parody trailer positions your game as entertaining and self-aware, which can significantly enhance player engagement and foster long-term loyalty through humor.

Identify the target elements you wish to spoof to create a successful parody trailer. This could range from popular game mechanics—like loot boxes or crafting systems—to overused storytelling clichés, such as the "chosen one" archetype or predictable plot twists. Consider current marketing strategies ripe for satire, like aggressive in-game purchasing models or overly dramatic trailers. By selecting these recognizable elements, you ensure your audience can relate to the humor and understand the context behind the jokes.

Embrace exaggerated visuals and absurd scenarios that underscore the ridiculousness of certain gaming practices. For instance, you might depict a character struggling comically with an overly complex crafting system or showcase a tutorial that takes an absurdly long time to explain a simple mechanic. Such moments encourage players to reflect on their own gaming experiences and the frustrations they may have encountered.

Paying close attention to the tone and pacing of your parody trailer is also essential. The rhythm should not only build anticipation but also deliver punchlines with precision. Quick cuts, whimsical voiceovers, and unexpected sound effects can enhance the comedic impact, transforming a simple joke into a memorable moment that resonates with viewers. Incorporating familiar gaming jargon, such as "grinding," "noob," or "power-up," alongside clever references to beloved franchises fosters camaraderie among your audience. It reinforces their sense of belonging to the gaming community.

Visuals are paramount in parody trailers, as they amplify humor and spotlight the absurdity of your chosen themes. Use vibrant colors, exaggerated character designs, and playful animations to captivate and hold viewers' attention from start to finish. If your game features a distinct art style, apply that same style to the parody elements. This visual cohesion reinforces the comedic aspects and strengthens brand identity. Adding humorous captions or on-screen text can further enhance the narrative, providing context for the jokes and adding layers to the humor.

Finally, leveraging community feedback and engagement is crucial in refining your parody trailers. Sharing a sneak peek or teaser with your gaming community can yield valuable insights into what truly resonates with your audience. Encouraging players to share their thoughts and reactions or even create their parody interpretations fosters a greater sense of community and extends the reach of your trailer. By actively engaging with your community, you enhance the effectiveness of your parody trailer and build a stronger, more resilient relationship— leading to increased player loyalty and participation in future humorous events or promotions.

Analyzing Successful Parodies in Gaming

Exploring successful parodies within the gaming industry illuminates the exciting potential of humor and satire in game design. Parody inherently imitates and amplifies existing works, often highlighting their absurdities and quirks. This engaging method entertains players and encourages them to reflect critically on the original content. Product managers can harness the creativity and humor found in these parodies to develop memorable prank game features that resonate with audiences, particularly during special occasions like April Fools' Day or other lighthearted in-game events.

A notable example of successful parody is the launch of "Fake Expansion Packs" by various games, which cleverly mimic popular game mechanics or themes while incorporating ludicrous, hyperbolic features. These expansions often include over-the-top items, nonsensical quests, or absurdly reimagined gameplay mechanics that players instantly recognize as exaggerated versions of the originals. By analyzing player reception and engagement with these expansions, product managers can uncover essential elements contributing to their success—such as optimal timing of the release, relatable content that aligns with player experiences, and clever marketing strategies that entice players. Effective parodies thrive on the audience's familiarity with the original material, making it crucial for developers to strike a balance between humor and recognition.

Humorous in-game events also present

a rich landscape for the exploration of parody. Games that introduce quirky challenges, satirical updates, or ironic game modes create memorable experiences that stand out in a crowded marketplace. For example, a game might temporarily modify its mechanics to parody a trending gameplay style—taking an increasingly popular mechanic and presenting it in a ridiculous light. This approach not only entertains players but also fosters a sense of reflection on the original trend's quirks. By scrutinizing the structure and execution of these events, product managers can craft playful challenges and temporary modes that not only engage players but also encourage community discussion and collective enjoyment.

Comedic game skins and fictional characters offer another vibrant avenue for successful parody. By designing exaggerated, caricatured versions of beloved characters or introducing skins that poke fun at popular gaming tropes, developers can elevate player enjoyment and enrich the gaming experience with layers of humor. The transformation of recognizable characters into whimsical counterparts sparks laughter and encourages sharing and dialogue within the gaming community. Product managers should actively explore the potential of incorporating these humorous elements into their games, promoting a joyful interaction with the content that enhances player connections and community bonding.

Ultimately, parody game trailers can serve as powerful tools for capturing audience attention and generating buzz. Successful trailers often employ comedic timing, absurd scenarios, and clever references to existing games, cultivating an instant connection with potential players. By embracing the qualities that resonate with their target audience, product managers can refine their marketing strategies to include similar techniques. A well-executed parody not only highlights the game's unique aspects but also presents a humorous perspective through which potential players can engage, fostering heightened interest and active participation in the gaming community.

Impact on Game Launches

The influence of compelling prank features on game launches is nothing short of remarkable, transforming player engagement and igniting community excitement. In games as a service, the careful timing and meticulous execution of these playful elements can create significant anticipation, drawing players back to the game and reigniting their passion. For instance, a well-crafted April Fools' joke—such as an unexpected in-game item or event that humorously exaggerates game mechanics—can create a viral sensation, inspiring players to share their experiences across social media platforms and increasing visibility for the game, thus attracting fresh audiences. This phenomenon strengthens the existing player community and invites new members through authentic word-of-mouth promotion.

Developers can establish a unique identity in a highly competitive landscape by embedding prank mechanics into a game's launch. Humorous in-game events, such as a silly celebration featuring oversized costumes or absurd challenges, challenge traditional gameplay norms and catch players off guard, providing memorable experiences. Introducing quirky characters endowed with bizarre traits—like a character who hilariously misinterprets instructions or a critter that disrupts gameplay comically—can spark unexpected dynamics and fuel conversations among players. Consequently, such innovative creativity can help a game stand out, cultivating a brand identity that resonates deeply with its audience.

Moreover, parody game trailers can redefine the narrative surrounding a game's launch. By skillfully blending humor with familiar tropes from established genres—like a mock horror game that features ridiculous jump scares—these trailers encapsulate the essence of beloved gaming conventions while playfully challenging them. This entertaining approach captivates potential players and fosters a joyous atmosphere that encourages them to view the game as a delightful and engaging journey worth exploring. A successful parody can generate significant buzz within the gaming community, making players eager to explore the game and its distinctive features.

Cleverly devised monetization strategies can further elevate the launch experience. Presenting ludicrous in-game items—like a ridiculously oversized sword that serves no practical purpose—while humorously critiquing standard pay-to-win models can shift player frustration into amusement, transforming typical complaints into opportunities for laughter. By embracing this playful narrative, developers can garner a more favorable reception from the player base and even boost sales of whimsical cosmetic items that enhance gameplay without compromising balance.

Finally, community challenges infused with prank elements are powerful tools for maintaining player engagement post-launch. Encouraging playful competitions—such as contests where players share their most ridiculous in-game moments or complete absurd challenges like "The Silly Dance-Off"—

fosters a spirit of camaraderie and collaboration. This keeps the game dynamic and lively and inspires players to return for ongoing adventures and updates. By weaving humor and creativity into community interactions, developers can nurture a vibrant ecosystem that thrives on shared joy and imagination, ultimately enhancing the longevity and success of their game.

Brainstorming Absurd Ideas in Game Development

Brainstorming absurd ideas is an essential and dynamic phase in crafting memorable and engaging prank game features that resonate deeply with players. For product managers in the gaming industry, particularly those focused on the games-as-a-service model, this creative exploration serves as a launchpad for devising unique experiences that surprise and delight users in unexpected ways. By fostering an environment encouraging imaginative thinking, teams can delve into unconventional avenues that challenge traditional design paradigms and spark innovation within the gaming community.

One effective method for generating these outlandish ideas is to host interactive brainstorming sessions where all participants are motivated to think outside the box. Establishing a playful atmosphere—where every idea, no matter how ludicrous it seems, is welcomed—empowers team members to explore wild concepts without the fear of judgment. For instance, imagine a game expansion pack featuring a quirky new character who is a sentient piece of furniture, like a wisecracking armchair, complete with an elaborate backstory that narrates its journey from a thrift store to becoming the game's hero. Such whimsical concepts inspire laughter and create excitement among players, encouraging them to be clever and explore the game in novel ways and develop a deeper connection with its world and characters.

Absurd ideas can also come to life through humorous in-game events engaging and entertaining players. Consider a monthly event where players must complete various tasks while being hilariously disrupted by surreal weather patterns, such as a torrential downpour of cats and dogs or an impromptu zombie parade staggering through their quest areas. These unpredictable events provide entertainment and create memorable experiences that players will fondly recount long after the features have wrapped up. The key is seamlessly integrating these absurdities with existing game mechanics, ensuring they feel like natural extensions of the core gameplay experience instead of isolated gimmicks.

Another promising avenue for absurd brainstorming is the exploration of satirical game updates. Product managers can cleverly parody prevalent gaming trends or industry practices through exaggerated features or mechanics that elicit laughter and spark conversation. For example, consider introducing a tongue-in-cheek monetization strategy that offers players the chance to purchase "invisible skins" or "pay-to-win" upgrades that are so outlandish—such as "literally fewer bullets" or "toxic positivity shields"—that they become a humorous commentary on real-world issues within the gaming industry. This approach entertains and actively engages the community in thoughtful discussions about the industry's direction and its often questionable practices.

Lastly, creating community challenges centered around absurd themes can enhance player involvement and foster a vibrant, connected gaming community. Envision a challenge that invites players to design the ridiculous character build, complete with outrageous abilities and comical backstories, or to create the funniest in-game scenario involving unexpected dialogues and interactions. By encouraging participation in these playful and imaginative activities, product managers can cultivate camaraderie and a sense of fun that entices players to return to the game. Ultimately, brainstorming absurd ideas aims to infuse humor and creativity into game design, making the gaming experience more enjoyable, engaging, and memorable for everyone involved.

Player Feedback and Iteration

Player feedback is the cornerstone for creating captivating features in prank games, particularly within the games-as-a-service model. By actively embracing insights and opinions from players, developers can gain a profound understanding of player preferences and the reception of various prank mechanics. Implementing effective feedback mechanisms—such as comprehensive surveys that gauge player satisfaction, dedicated community forums for open discussions, and in-game prompts that encourage immediate reactions—invites players to share their experiences in real-time. Product managers should rigorously foster these channels for player input, ensuring they remain closely connected to the community's reactions and sentiments. This active engagement is essential for shaping the evolution of their prank game offerings in a way that feels organic and player-driven.

Iterative design is vital in honing prank features that genuinely resonate with an engaged audience. After collecting and analyzing feedback, product managers delve into thoughtful analysis, identifying trends and common themes that inform meaningful adjustments to gameplay mechanics. For example, suppose a particular comedic game skin unveils mixed reviews. In that case, some players may appreciate its novelty while others criticize its functionality—digging deeper into player commentary can reveal which elements players cherish or critique most. This insight can steer future iterations in a direction that amplifies player enjoyment. Thus, iteration becomes more than just a series of tasks; it evolves into a continuous, enriching cycle that consistently boosts player engagement and satisfaction over time.

In the dynamic realm of humorous in-game events and satirical updates, the timing and execution of features become paramount. Player feedback can illuminate whether a particular event feels timely and well-integrated into the gaming landscape or if it ultimately falls flat. For instance, aligning a prank event with significant real-world occasions—like a holiday or a major cultural phenomenon—can foster a deeper emotional connection with players. Product managers must cultivate agility and readiness to pivot their approaches based on insights gained, refining event mechanics or introducing innovative features that resonate with player expectations and current cultural trends. This adaptability is important to keeping the game relevant, engaging, and appropriately responsive to the evolving tastes of its audience.

The significance of community challenges within prank games is undeniable and can profoundly enhance the player experience. These challenges thrive on active player participation and enthusiasm, facilitating an environment of collaboration and competition. Product managers can keenly observe player responses and engagement metrics to uncover specific elements that ignite their audience's motivation and interest. Constructive feedback can inspire the development of new, absurd game features or whimsical monetization strategies that further enhance the joyful spirit of the game. Recognizing and understanding community dynamics allows for strategically introducing features that promote impactful engagement, thus nurturing a vibrant and interactive player base.

Ultimately, weaving player feedback and iterative practices into the design process of prank games is essential for crafting genuinely delightful experiences. By championing player input to its fullest, product managers can fine-tune game features, ensuring they are aligned with community expectations while entirely celebrating the playful essence of the game. This iteration, grounded in genuine feedback, not only enriches the immediate player experience but also lays a strong foundation for the long-term success of games as a service. In this ever-evolving digital entertainment landscape, embracing player perspectives paves the way for innovative and entertaining prank game mechanics that continually surprise and delight audiences, fostering an enduring relationship between players and creators.

Exploring Outlandish Monetization Ideas

Exploring outlandish monetization ideas can ignite a fresh and invigorating perspective on engaging audiences while amplifying the enjoyment of prank game mechanics. As product managers navigating the vibrant landscape of the gaming industry, mastering the delicate dance between humor and profitability is crucial. By venturing into unconventional monetization strategies, teams can create unforgettable experiences that resonate deeply with players, leaving an indelible mark on their gaming journey. This subchapter embarks on an insightful journey through a spectrum of innovative concepts that amuse and generate revenue in unexpected and delightful ways.

One captivating approach is the introduction of fake expansion packs that promise absurd and whimsical features, catching players' attention through sheer silliness. Envision a "Giant Hamster Wheel" mode, where players tackle oversized, cartoonish obstacles in a fantastical race against imaginary foes like "Invisible Dragons" or "Ninja Squirrels." With exaggerated claims —such as "Experience the thrill of running 50% faster while being chased by pretend monsters!"—alongside vibrant graphics and playful descriptions, developers can enthrall players while cleverly guiding them toward purchasing a seemingly ridiculous addition. This strategy harnesses the element of surprise and taps into the willingness of players to invest in the absurd, enriching their overall gaming experience and ensuring they come back for more laughs.

In-game events designed for laughter can also emerge as remarkably effective monetization tools. Imagine organizing a "Prankster's Paradise" weekend event, where players earn virtual currency and exclusive rewards through participation in outrageous challenges—such as dressing characters in wild costumes inspired by television sitcoms or completing delightfully silly tasks like juggling virtual pies. Offering limited-time, humorous in-game items—like oversized rubber chickens or comically exaggerated mustaches—for purchase can further entice participation. This fosters a vibrant community as players share their unique experiences, stream gameplay using hashtag challenges, and showcase imaginative creations on social media, leading to organic promotion and increased sales.

Another inventive monetization method is creating fictional characters that embody absurdity, ensuring they leave a lasting impression on the players. Picture introducing a character known as the "Master of Awkward Situations," who offers a series of ridiculous quests with hilarious, unexpected outcomes— like accidentally turning an enemy into a bouncy castle. Allowing players to purchase unique skins or quirky accessories for these characters, such as oversized glasses or mismatched socks, capitalizes on the allure of customization while keeping the tone light-hearted and engaging. This deepens player investment and opens doors for additional revenue streams through character-related merchandise, like plush toys or themed apparel.

Finally, parody game trailers can serve as a unique monetization strategy while captivating the audience's interest. By crafting trailers that cleverly spoof popular game trends—like exaggerated battle cries or overly dramatic animations—developers can rapidly draw attention and spark interest among potential players. These cleverly orchestrated trailers, paired with promotional offers for in-game items or features aligned with the parody theme, provide amusement and a sense of camaraderie within the gaming community. Embracing humor in marketing efforts allows teams to harness the power of satire, enhancing their monetization strategies in a fun and relatable manner.

In conclusion, exploring outlandish monetization ideas within prank games unveils numerous innovative avenues for product managers to consider. By integrating fake expansion packs, humorous in-game events, absurd characters, and comedic trailers into their strategy, deseigners can create engaging experiences that resonate with players while effectively driving revenue. The key lies in understanding the audience's appetite for humor and crafting strategies that entertain and cultivate a strong sense of community around the game. Embracing these playful concepts has the potential to lead to pioneering monetization strategies that truly shine in an increasingly crowded market.

Balancing Profit and Player Experience

Balancing profit and player experience is a crucial cornerstone of game design, particularly when integrating prank game features into the "Games as a Service" model. To generate sustainable revenue, developers must implement thoughtful monetization strategies that do not compromise the quality of player experience. A game's enduring success relies on a delicate equilibrium between these two aspects, which necessitates a deep understanding of player expectations, preferences, and the overall impact of design choices on player engagement and profitability.

Incorporating prank mechanics into game design requires a nuanced understanding of player psychology. Players are often attracted to the delight and laughter that emerge from surprises within the game experience. However, frustration can arise if these playful elements disrupt gameplay or seem unjust. To mitigate this, product managers should introduce humorous features—such as fake expansion packs, pranks that temporarily alter in-game mechanics, or satirical updates designed to mimic legitimate content—in a manner that respects the integrity of the core gaming experience. Limited-time events marked as playful or absurd allow players to engage with content on their own terms, enhancing satisfaction while promoting revenue generation.

Moreover, creating comedic characters, skins, or even entire zones can serve as a lucrative revenue stream and a means to enrich the player experience. To maintain coherence, it is essential to align these features with the game's aesthetic and narrative. Absurd game elements should feel like organic extensions of the game world, offering players unexpected delights while generating interest and sales. For instance, introducing a fictional character that parodies a well-known trope within the game can add a humorous twist, captivating players and fueling enjoyment and community engagement.

Community involvement emerges as a powerful strategy for harmonizing profit with player experience. By designing playful challenges or events that encourage collaboration—such as cooperative quests or competitions—product managers can harness the collective enthusiasm of the player base. These events, especially when linked to limited-time offers or exclusive in-game items, foster a sense of belonging and attachment while promoting monetization. Furthermore, integrating player feedback into the development process can refine these experiences, ensuring they align with the audience's desire for fun, humor, and meaningful interaction.

Achieving a successful balance between profit and player experience demands ongoing analysis and iterative development. Product managers must be vigilant regarding player reactions to prank game mechanics and remain flexible, ready to adapt strategies as necessary. Developers can enhance player retention by experimenting with diverse monetization approaches, such as seasonal events or subscription models that introduce new comedic elements. Prioritizing the player experience while keeping business goals in mind enables designers to cultivate a vibrant gaming ecosystem that not only delights players but also drives profits, ensuring the sustainability of prank game features in the ever-evolving gaming industry landscape.

Case Studies of Unique Monetization

Examining unique monetization strategies in prank games reveals the profound impact of creativity in engaging players while generating significant revenue. One example is the integration of whimsical in-game features, such as a "Pet Rock" that players can purchase for a nominal fee. This seemingly useless item cleverly embodies the game's humor and absurdity while serving as an innovative monetization vehicle. The novelty and irony of investing in an item stripped of functional utility captivate players, demonstrating how a lighthearted approach can inspire unexpected sales and enhance player retention.

Another compelling case involves the implementation of parody expansion packs that cleverly mock traditional downloadable content (DLC) offerings. For instance, a game might introduce a fictional pack titled "The Ultimate Adventure: The Quest for More Quests," which includes laughable elements like a character that can only walk backward and a collection of weapons that hilariously shoot confetti. This absurdity not only entertains players but also encourages them to share their unique experiences on social media platforms, effectively promoting the game and expanding its reach. Such strategies cultivate a vibrant community, leading to increased revenue streams through sales and ensuring a solidified market presence.

Humorous in-game events also serve as potent monetization tools. Consider a game that celebrates "National Pretend You're a Pirate Day," inviting players to purchase themed cosmetic items like eye patches, inflatable swords, and pirate hats. By creating a time-limited event that sparks nostalgia and excitement, developers tap into players' desires for unique and memorable experiences. This fusion of humor and urgency fosters a joyous atmosphere, increasing players' likelihood of investing in the event for full engagement, thereby driving in-game purchases.

Moreover, comedic game skins present a significant revenue opportunity. One illustrative case features a game where players can buy skins transforming their characters into exaggerated caricatures of iconic figures from popular culture or fictional realms. Imagine a superhero reinvented as a whimsical version of themselves, complete with humorous animations that bring comic relief to gameplay. These skins not only enhance the game's visual variety but also ignite community sharing and interaction, amplifying visibility and sales across diverse platforms.

Lastly, parody game trailers have proven to be an exceptional method for attracting attention to various monetization strategies. For example, a game might release a trailer that humorously exaggerates its features, playfully claiming players can "become the ultimate couch potato" through their unique gaming experience. This engaging marketing approach generates buzz and piques interest among potential players, ultimately resulting in heightened pre-launch sales and in-game purchases. By skillfully harnessing humor and satire, developers can create unforgettable promotional content that resonates deeply with players, fostering long-term loyalty and engagement.

Designing Engaging Community Challenges

Designing engaging community challenges is crucial for igniting active participation and enhancing player interaction within prank games' dynamic and often whimsical realm. These challenges transcend mere entertainment; they cultivate a profound sense of belonging among players, transforming the gaming experience into one filled with camaraderie and shared laughter. Product managers aiming to implement these initiatives must ensure that they resonate with the humor, creativity, and absurdity characteristic of prank games. The challenge design must effectively balance imaginative concepts with practical execution, enabling players to quickly comprehend and immerse themselves in the activities while feeling a genuine thrill from the game's unique elements.

One effective strategy is to align challenges with seasonal events or culturally significant moments, particularly around the playful spirit of April Fools' Day. Product managers can craft imaginative challenges inviting players to showcase their most outlandish and humorous in-game pranks. For example, players could be tasked with creating delightfully absurd scenarios featuring beloved long-standing game characters or generating comedic game skins that amplify the humor, such as outlandish costumes that transform characters in unexpected ways. Utilizing elements of surprise and the lively, playful nature of these events can significantly enhance player engagement and help forge a vibrant community atmosphere filled with enthusiasm and laughter.

Incorporating social elements into these community challenges can further amplify engagement. Encouraging players to share their entertaining experiences on platforms like Twitter, Instagram, or within the game's community forums elevates the visibility and excitement surrounding these challenges. Moreover, promoting collaborative efforts, where players work together to achieve outrageous goals or tackle in-game tasks that require teamwork and creativity—such as forming prank squads—strengthens community bonds and boosts player retention. Participants often eagerly anticipate the next thrilling challenge, motivated by the shared experience and collective humor.

Additionally, utilizing satirical game updates as a backdrop for community challenges adds an engaging layer of humor that resonates deeply with players. Product managers can create fictional game expansion packs or amusing parody trailers that humorously critique familiar gaming tropes, inviting players to participate in challenges that reflect these entertaining updates. Participants could be asked to humorously parody trending gaming mechanics or poke fun at overused monetization strategies through in-game actions or creative content, resulting in a rich and engaging experience that connects with the community's shared understanding and humor.

Finally, measuring the success of these community challenges is vital for ongoing improvement and development. Gathering feedback from enthusiastic participants through surveys or community discussions and analyzing engagement metrics—such as participation rates, social media shares, and player retention statistics—offers invaluable insights into which elements yield excitement and which may need refinement. This critical data supports the iterative design of future challenges, ensuring they remain fresh, innovative, and appealing. By fostering a dynamic cycle of idea generation and responsiveness to player feedback, product managers can create a vibrant ecosystem of engaging community challenges that inspire joy, interaction, and a yearning for delightful experiences.

Fostering a Fun Community Spirit

Cultivating a fun community spirit is vital for any game, particularly in prank games and humorous content. Product managers must recognize that player engagement and retention significantly hinge on the connections formed, not only with the game itself but also among players within the community. By establishing an atmosphere that celebrates humor, creativity, and shared experiences, product managers can nurture a vibrant community eager to actively contribute to the game's evgame'sn.

This lively atmosphere can be invigorated through various features, such as in-game events that promote collaboration and friendly competition. These events enable players to forge meaningful bonds over shared moments of hilarity. A particularly effective method for enhancing community spirit is humorous in-game events that align with real-world celebrations, such as the widely commemorated April Fool's Day. During this occasion, implementing whimsical updates or introducing absurd game mechanics can resonate deeply with players' desires for lightheartedness and entertainment.

For instance, product managers might consider temporary features that turn established gameplay conventions on their heads—such as chaotically swapping character abilities or introducing an unconventional "reverse" mode where players experience the game from an entirely different perspective. Such inventive events do not only amuse players, but they also create memorable moments that encourage them to share their unique experiences and strategies, thereby enriching their overall gaming journey and contributing to a collective narrative.

Moreover, incorporating fictional characters or outrageous skins tailored for these events can significantly heighten player engagement. Product managers should explore introducing characters that embody the essence of the prank, complete with exaggerated traits, whimsical designs, and quirky backstories that players can rally around. For example, a character like "Jester Joe," known for his comically erratic behavior and wild antics, might become a beloved mascot for events, seamlessly intertwining his narrative with the stories players create. This shared lore fosters a more profound connection with the game and among community members, sparking lively discussions and interactions on various platforms, including social media and community forums.

Another compelling strategy involves organizing playful community challenges that encourage players to tap into their creativity within the game world. Product managers can harness the community's inventive spirit by motivating users to create and share their own absurd content—be it fan art, comedic videos, or imaginative mock trailers. For example, a challenge prompting players to design the silliest game skin or the most outlandish in-game scenario can lead to a wealth of creative submissions. This provides a stage for players to showcase their humor and incentivizes organic growth. Participants eagerly share their creations across social media channels, inviting new players to join the fun.

The sense of achievement and recognition tied to these challenges fosters a positive feedback loop. Players who participate and receive accolades or shout-outs within the game feel valued, making them more likely to engage with the content and the community, thereby fortifying their connections with both. Finally, leveraging satirical game updates and outlandish monetization strategies can bolster a fun community spirit. Product managers can intentionally push the envelope of player expectations by presenting updates that humorously parody common industry trends —such as absurdly exaggerated loot boxes or whimsical subscription memberships that poke fun at ongoing market practices.

This self-aware approach provokes laughter while inviting players to discuss and critique these features light-heartedly, fostering dialogue that further strengthens the community. Ultimately, nurturing a fun community spirit through these diverse, thoughtfully implemented methods can lead to a more engaged and loyal player base, amplifying prank games' overall success and longevity. By combining innovation, creativity, and a touch of humor, these games can remain delightful and relevant for all.

Measuring Participation and Success in Prank Game Mechanics

Measuring participation and success in prank game mechanics is an exhilarating journey that captures the essence of player engagement and satisfaction. By establishing clear, quantifiable metrics, we unlock the potential to deeply understand how our audience interacts with the whimsical features we create. For example, tracking participation rates in humorous in-game events, such as limited-time challenges or seasonal festivities, analyzing player engagement during targeted April Fools' Day promotions, and assessing the popularity of satirical updates and patches illuminate the paths our players enjoy. Key performance indicators (KPIs), which include active user counts, average session lengths, and player retention rates, provide invaluable insights into how well these playful elements resonate with our community.

Collecting player feedback through various channels and fostering community engagement reveal the heart of our game's experience. Utilizing structured surveys, interactive polls, and dedicated forums allows us to gather a rich tapestry of qualitative data reflecting players' interactions with prank mechanics—ranging from humorous fake expansion packs to ludicrous in-game features. This feedback is a guiding light for product managers, enabling them to identify which aspects of the game spark joy and which might require reimagining. Monitoring social media interactions, analyzing player-generated content, such as memes and videos, and engaging with the community on platforms like Discord also enriches our understanding of the features' success and players' sentiments.

In-game metrics enhance our analysis

of success even further. By rigorously tracking player participation in community challenges, such as collaborative quests that allow players to earn exclusive rewards or engaging with parody trailers that spoof popular gaming trends, we can unearth valuable trends in player behavior and preferences. Implementing A/B testing for different prank mechanics—for instance, comparing the uptake of absurd in-game skins and outrageous monetization strategies like humorous loot boxes—empowers product managers to refine game designs. This data-driven approach fine-tunes game elements, ultimately enhancing player satisfaction while deepening emotional connections with the game.

Retention and monetization play pivotal roles in the ongoing success of our prank features. Ideally, the seamless integration of humor within gameplay leads to higher player retention; when players find genuine enjoyment in lighthearted experiences, they are significantly more inclined to return for repeat play. Furthermore, examining the effects of whimsical monetization strategies, such as seasonal sales featuring comedic character skins or exaggerated bundles, on player spending behavior reveals how effectively these prank features bolster our game's financial health. Striking a balance between humor and monetization is essential for maintaining player trust while achieving our business goals.

Ultimately, measuring participation and success in prank game mechanics is a dynamic, ongoing process that adapts to player feedback and market trends. As player preferences evolve, product managers must remain flexible and responsive to this feedback loop. By employing a robust blend of quantitative metrics—such as sales data and engagement statistics—and qualitative insights from player interactions, we can achieve a comprehensive understanding of our prank features' performance. This proactive effort not only enriches the player experience but also drives the long-term success of our game in a vibrant and competitive gaming market, ensuring it remains a beloved title among players.

Trends in Gaming and Humor

The gaming landscape is a dynamic canvas of creativity, where humor plays a vital role in its evolution. As product managers, embracing the current trends in gaming and humor allows us to craft engaging prank game features that resonate deeply with players. One remarkable trend is the rise of "games as a service," a model where developers consistently update content to captivate players. This approach opens the door to numerous opportunities for infusing humor—such as timed events or limited-time features that delightfully subvert player expectations. For example, April Fool's Day is a prime opportunity for game developers to unleash their creativity. It surprises players with imaginative designs like whimsical character skins or absurd in-game mechanics that play on classic tropes.

Prank game mechanics are increasingly prevalent, with developers exploring innovative avenues to weave humor into gameplay. By incorporating unexpected character abilities, such as a character that can momentarily revert to a previous version of themselves or whimsical in-game physics that defies traditional gravity, we can create laugh-out-loud moments that elicit genuine joy. These captivating mechanics do more than merely engage players; they inspire social sharing, as players eagerly showcase their entertaining experiences on social media platforms and streaming services, organically boosting the game's visibility and enhancing player retention.

The emergence of fake game expansion packs is a brilliant strategic move for developers aiming to inject humor into their offerings. These satirical packs playfully parody popular franchises or current gaming trends, offering a humorous twist on what players might expect from a legitimate expansion. For example, an exaggerated pack might introduce ludicrous character designs— like a hero with a comically oversized weapon or a villain whose power comes from failing spectacularly. By embracing nonsensical storylines that poke fun at industry norms, we can engage our audience with creativity and surprise, giving them an experience that lingers long after logging off.

Humorous in-game events and satirical updates are essential for maintaining player interest and fostering community engagement. Whether through seasonal celebrations like a Winter Holiday that features comedic challenges or spontaneous in-game disruptions—such as a character going rogue and creating chaos—these events infuse life and excitement into the gaming experience. Imagine a whimsical in-game holiday filled with bizarre collectibles and ludicrous tasks, energizing our player base while allowing fictional characters with outlandish personalities to foster personal connections through shared humor.

Finally, the trend of introducing absurd game features and ridiculous monetization strategies paves the way for playful innovation. Developers can create a unique blend of humor and marketing brilliance by intentionally designing over-the-top features that challenge conventional expectations while critiquing existing monetization practices—such as a fictional in-game purchase that humorously famines resources. By infusing humor into these aspects, we can cultivate a lively community atmosphere that encourages players to engage meaningfully with the game and each other in delightful, unexpected ways, ultimately enriching their overall gaming experience.

Embracing the Next Wave of Pranks

Embracing the next wave of pranks requires a strategic mindset that harmonizes with the core principles of game design while capturing the joy and whimsy that resonate deeply with players. Product managers embark on a comprehensive research journey, delving into various prank types that have flourished within their own games and across the broader gaming industry. This entails a meticulous analysis of player feedback, engagement metrics, and participation data from past April Fools' events, uncovering invaluable insights into what strikes a chord with the audience. For instance, by reviewing successful pranks from competitors and predecessors, they can identify patterns that lead to high player satisfaction and memorable experiences.

Moreover, this exploration extends to a thoughtful examination of community reactions to different prank mechanics, aligning these findings with current gaming trends and the dynamic preferences of diverse player demographics. Understanding which styles of humor resonate with specific audiences—be it playful absurdity, clever satire, or harmless mischief—enables the development of tailored prank experiences that feel personal and engaging.

Fostering a spirit of collaboration among cross-functional teams is crucial to this endeavor. Product managers cultivate an environment where innovative ideas can flourish by involving developers, designers, artists, and marketers early in the planning phase. For example, brainstorming workshops can lead to the generation of concepts that effectively blend humor with gameplay mechanics, ensuring that prank implementations elevate the overall player experience rather than detract from it. The diverse perspectives of each team member contribute to a richer, more authentic product, firmly grounding it within the game's unique universe and lore.

Timing and delivering these prank features require careful consideration, as they are pivotal in the overall impact on players. Seasonal events, such as April Fools' Day, Halloween, or mid-summer celebrations, provide the perfect backdrop for launching new updates that captivate players' attention and create a buzz. Striking a balance between surprise and delight is vital; prank features should invite joy and laughter, ensuring players feel included and entertained rather than bewildered or frustrated. This could involve teasing upcoming pranks through cryptic hints or engaging trailers that build anticipation without revealing too much.

Integrating player-generated content can significantly amplify the impact of prank features. By inviting the community to submit their prank ideas or vote on potential game updates, developers foster a sense of ownership and investment among players. This participatory approach deepens connections between the game and its community and ignites genuine excitement leading up to the launch of new prank elements. Events such as community contests or social media challenges further bolster engagement and creativity.

Finally, evaluating the success of pranks post-launch is pivotal for refining future strategies. Gathering comprehensive data on player engagement, retention rates, and community sentiment provides insights into how effectively the prank features resonated with the audience. Product managers can gather actionable feedback that guides iterative improvements by conducting surveys, analyzing gameplay data, and actively monitoring social media reactions. This continuous feedback loop empowers product teams to enhance their approach, leading to more engaging, entertaining, and humorous content in future waves of pranks.

By wholeheartedly preparing for the next wave of pranks, product managers can craft unforgettable experiences that amplify player enjoyment and strengthen community bonds. This cultivation of a vibrant and interactive gaming world fosters a sense of belonging among players, making every prank not just a moment of humor but a lasting memory in their gaming journey.